Apel, Melanie Ann

**Land and Resources of
Ancient Greece**

LAND AND RESOURCES OF ANCIENT GREECE

MELANIE ANN APEL

The Rosen Publishing Group's
PowerKids Press™
PRIMARY SOURCE

New York

For Hayden, Aidan, Ashwin, Dylan, Emmy, Ellie, Lucy, Inman, and Jack

Published in 2004 by The Rosen Publishing Group, Inc.
29 East 21st Street, New York, NY 10010

First Edition

Editors: John Cassel and Joanne Randolph
Book Design: Michael de Guzman
Layout Design: Kim Sonsky
Photo Researcher: Peter Tomlinson

Photo Credits: Cover (center), pp. 11 (left), 19 © Gianni Dagli Orti/CORBIS; cover (right), p. 12 (top and bottom right) Scala/Art Resource, NY; p. 4 The Art Archive/Dagli Orti; p. 4 (inset) The Metropolitan Museum of Art, Gift of Norbert Schimmel Trust, 1989 (1989.281.69) Photograph © 1992 The Metropolitan Museum of Art; p. 7 © Mick Roessler/Index Stock Imagery; p. 7 (inset) © Hubert Stadler/CORBIS; pp. 8,16 Erich Lessing/Art Resource, NY; pp. 11 (right) Réunion des Musées Nationaux/Art Resource, NY; p. 12 (left) The Metropolitan Museum of Art, Gift of Norbert Schimmel Trust, 1989 (1989.281.49) Photograph © 1991 The Metropolitan Museum of Art; p. 15 SEF/Art Resource, NY; p. 17 Museum of Cycladic and Ancient Greek Art, Athens, Greece/Bridgeman Art Library; p. 20 © CORBIS; p. 20 (inset) Wadsworth Atheneum, Hartford, Gift of J. Pierpont Morgan; p. 22 © Roger Wood/CORBIS.

Apel, Melanie Ann.
   Land and resources of ancient Greece/Melanie Ann Apel. 1st ed.
      p. cm.— (Primary sources of ancient civilizations. Greece)
   Includes bibliographical references and index.
   Contents: The geography of ancient Greece—Climate—Agriculture—Diet in ancient Greece—Mining for metals—Forced to trade—The Mediterranean Sea—The sea and trade—Two citystates—Thousands of years.
   ISBN 0-8239-6769-7 (lib. bdg.)—ISBN 0-8239-8937-2 (paperback)
1. Greece—Civilization—To 146 B.C.—Juvenile literature. 2. Greece—Geography—Juvenile literature. 3. Natural resources—Greece—History—To 1500—Juvenile literature. [1. Greece—Civilization—To 146 B.C. 2. Greece—Geography. 3. Natural resources—Greece.] I. Title. II. Series.
   DF78.A63 2004
   913.8—dc21
                                                                    2002153728

Manufactured in the United States of America

Contents

The Geography of Ancient Greece   5

Climate   6

Agriculture   9

Diet in Ancient Greece   10

Mining for Metals   13

Forced to Trade   14

The Mediterranean Sea   17

The Sea and Trade   18

Two City-States   21

Thousands of Years   22

Glossary   23

Index   24

Primary Sources   24

Web Sites   24

The Geography of Ancient Greece

The geography of Greece shaped the civilization that grew there thousands of years ago. Greece is a peninsula and a group of islands that reach from southeastern Europe into the Mediterranean Sea. The sea and its resources drew much of the population to settle on the coast and to rely on fishing and trade for food. Most of Greece is mountainous and rocky. Only 18 percent of its land could be farmed. Ancient Greeks had to rely on other industries, such as shipbuilding. The mountains that divided ancient Greece made communication and travel among communities hard. This division contributed to the formation of the polis, or independent city-state.

Ancient Greece consisted of a peninsula and many small islands.
◀ Inset: *Soldiers ride dolphins on this urn. Many ancient Greeks lived near the Mediterranean Sea, which was full of such sea life.*

Climate

The climate of ancient Greece varied with the region. The three main regions were the coast, the lowlands, and the mountains. The lowlands and the coast had long, dry summers. The sea cooled the air to about 75°F (23.9°C). The short, wet winters averaged from 20 to 50 inches (50.8–127 cm) of rain per year. The average winter temperature was 40°F (4.4°C). The mountains were colder and snowy. The snow, when it melted, supplied the rivers and streams with water. The melted snow also allowed mountainside pastures to grow. Pastures did not exist in lower regions with summer droughts. Shepherds took flocks from the lowlands to the mountains to eat the grass in spring and summer.

Mount Olympus is the tallest mountain in Greece. Streams in the mountains flow with water from melting snow. ▶

Animals could graze in mountain pastures, such as this one near the town of Lindos.

7

Above: *Ancient Greeks pick bunches of grapes in the painting on this vase. Ancient Greeks harvested grapes in September. They used the grapes to make wine.* Right: *The Greeks served wine from jars such as this one.*

Agriculture

The economy of ancient Greece relied heavily on agriculture, even though the rocky soil and summer droughts made planting crops hard. The long summers and nearly 300 days of sunshine each year were ideal for growing olives, grapes, figs, and grains. The Greeks ate these crops and traded them with nearby places, such as Syria, Turkey, and Egypt. Olives and grapes were the best crops to sell. Grapes were used to make wine and were also used in cooking. Olives were pressed into olive oil. The Greeks used olive oil in cooking and as a base for soaps and perfumes. These items were made for personal use and for trade. Barley became the main cereal crop because it grew well with little rain.

Diet in Ancient Greece

Along with olives, figs, barley, and grapes, some other foods also grew fairly well in the land. These were onions, cabbages, melons, pumpkins, lentils, and garlic. The pastures in the mountains allowed people living there to raise sheep, cattle, goats, and pigs. Many families in ancient Greece also raised chickens. This meant families could produce meat and dairy products. Eating the crops produced in the lowlands and the fish provided by the sea, the Greeks in ancient times had a fairly balanced diet. Historians report that the people of ancient Greece ate mainly bread, goat cheese, olives, figs, wine, honey, eggs, fish, and occasionally meat.

In this painting, which dates from the sixteenth century B.C., a Greek man holds fish he has caught. Fish were an important part of the diet of the ancient Greeks.

A farmer stands behind his oxen in this statue from the sixth century B.C. The oxen pull a plow to break up the soil and to dig a long hole in which the farmer will plant seeds.

11

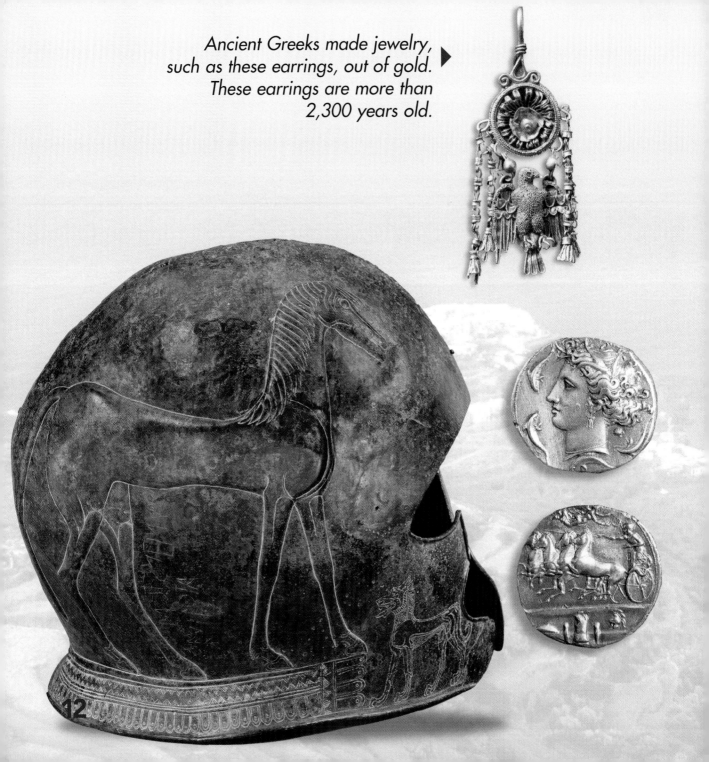

Ancient Greeks made jewelry,
such as these earrings, out of gold.
These earrings are more than
2,300 years old.

12

Mining for Metals

Each region in ancient Greece offered different natural resources. The mountains of Thrace in northern Greece and the island of Sífnos, for example, had rich supplies of gold and silver. Gold and silver were valuable for trade and were also used to craft jewelry and to make coins. Greece also had supplies of iron ore. Iron was used for tools and weapons, and it was also important for trade. At Laurium, near Athens, the men worked in the mines, bringing up lead ore. Cyprus was known for copper. Copper was used to craft armor, weapons, tools, vases, razors, and jewelry in ancient Greece.

◄ Left: *This bronze helmet was made on the Greek island Crete around 600 B.C. Bronze is made by melting and mixing copper and tin.* Right: *Ancient Greeks made coins such as these, out of silver.*

Forced to Trade

The ancient Greeks had plenty of limestone and marble, which they used for buildings and sculptures. For the most part, though, the resources available to each region of Greece varied. Some places were lucky and had fertile farmlands as well as pastures and minable mineral deposits. Other places had only one or none of these resources available. Most regions needed to trade items of which they had a lot for the products they did not have. For instance, Corinth had fertile land in the west, which produced barley, wheat, and grapes. The rest of its land was barren. However, its location allowed Corinth to trade by sea and by land for items the people needed to live.

Ancient Greeks used their plentiful marble in sculptures such as this lion from Naxos, a Greek island. The sculpture dates from 575 B.C. ▶

The Mediterranean Sea

The Mediterranean Sea was the greatest resource available to the ancient Greeks. It provided not only a supply of fish but also a way to reach other regions. Ancient Greeks sailed to the Greek islands as well as to neighboring lands, such as Egypt. In ancient Greece, nearly 700 small communities stood within 40 miles (64.4 km) of the water's edge. These coastal communities were often wealthier than were settlements inland. The Mediterranean Sea gave people a way to more communities with which they could trade. The Greeks on the coast could also control trade and charge ships a fee to come into their harbors.

The ancient Greek coastal city of Miletus was a large and powerful center of trade located in what is now the country of Turkey.

The Sea and Trade

Greeks relied on ships to move cargo easily and quickly because the rocky land and the many mountains made overland travel hard and slow. Many ports were created to take advantage of this need. Close to Crete, on the Sea of Crete, was a port called Amnisos. Greece made important trades with nearby countries, such as Syria and Egypt, at this port. They traded for papyrus, cattle, dyes, gold, wool, and many other things. The port of Amnisos had a very large population because of the successful trade. People living inland often sought new opportunities for wealth by moving to the coastal regions and ports such as Amnisos.

This wall painting from the Greek island of Thera is more than 3,000 years old. It shows a fleet arriving in a port. The settlement at Thera was built on cliffs almost 1,312 feet (400 m) above the sea. ▶

The Spartan warrior in this sculpture wears his military cloak.

Two City-States

Athens and Sparta, two major Greek city-states, show how geography and resources shape societies. Athens had a harbor and fertile land. It grew cash crops such as olives and grapes. Athenians had a peaceful relationship of trade with neighboring city-states. Athenians grew wealthier and Athens became a democracy. Athens was known for its sophistication and culture. Sparta was not located by the sea, so trade was hard. It also lacked fertile land. Sparta marched into other Greek city-states to take their land and wealth. Every Spartan boy was sent to military school by age seven to train for this lifestyle. Spartans were known for simplicity and discipline.

◀ *The Athenian Parthenon was built in the seventh century B.C. and still stands today. The Parthenon was a temple for Athena, the goddess of war and wisdom, for whom Athens was named.*

Thousands of Years

Greece, with all its small islands, tall mountains, and deep, generous waters, has been home to many people for more than 4,000 years. Ancient Greece was a land of farmers, fishers, and merchants. City-states used the land and the sea to meet their needs. The Greek civilization flourished, and its city-states made lasting contributions through their beautiful art and buildings, as well as in science, math, and philosophy. Today the people of Greece continue to contribute to the world community from their small peninsula in the Mediterranean Sea.

This mosaic from the House of Dolphins on the Greek island of Delos shows a man riding a dolphin. Dolphins have swum in the Mediterranean Sea and have been a sign of protection and good luck since ancient times. ▶

Glossary

communication (kuh-myoo-nih-KAY-shun) The sharing of facts or feelings.

culture (KUL-chur) The beliefs, practices, and art of a group of people.

democracy (dih-MAH-kruh-see) A government that is run by the people who live under it.

discipline (DIH-sih-plin) Training or developing by teaching and exercise.

droughts (DROWTS) Periods of dryness that cause damage to crops.

fertile (FER-tul) Good for making and growing things.

industries (IN-dus-treez) Moneymaking businesses in which many people work and make money producing a particular product.

lowlands (LOH-landz) Lands that are lower and flatter than the land around them.

papyrus (puh-PY-rus) A type of paper, on which ancient peoples wrote, made from the leaves of the papyrus plant.

pastures (PAS-churz) Pieces of land where animals eat plants.

peninsula (peh-NIN-suh-luh) An area of land surrounded by water on three sides.

philosophy (fih-LAH-suh-fee) A system of thought that tries to understand the nature of that which is real.

resources (REE-ors-ez) Supplies or sources of energy or useful material.

sophistication (suh-fih-stih-KAY-shun) The state of being highly advanced in knowledge.

temperature (TEM-pruh-cher) How hot or cold something is.

Index

A
Athens, Greece, 21

C
city-state(s), 5, 21–22
Corinth, Greece, 14
crop(s), 9–10, 21

D
droughts, 6, 9

E
economy, 9

F
fishing, 5

I
industries, 5

L
lowlands, 6, 10

M
Mediterranean Sea, 5
mountains, 5–6, 10, 13, 18, 22

R
resource(s), 5, 13–14, 17

S
Sífnos, Greece, 13
Sparta, Greece, 21

T
trade, 5, 9, 13, 17–18

Primary Sources

Cover, title page. Entrance of fleet into port. Fresco. Thirteenth century B.C. From island of Thera. National Archaeological Museum, Athens. **Bottom right.** Greek plate with fish. Museo Archeologico. Taranto, Italy. **Page 4.** Greece and Aegean islands, from *Theatrum Orbis Terrarum*, Abraham Ortelius, 1570. **Inset.** Psykter (vase for cooling wine). Terra-cotta. Attributed to Oltos. Circa 520–510 B.C. Metropolitan Museum of Art, New York. **Page 8. Right.** Rhodian oenochos (wine jar) with animal decor, deer and swans. Seventh century B.C. Musée du Louvre, Paris. **Page 11. Left.** Fisher. Sixteenth century B.C. **Right.** Farmer plowing with oxen. Terra-cotta. 600–550 B.C. From Thebes. Musée du Louvre, Paris. **Page 12. Top right.** Gold earrings. Circa 330–327 B.C. Hellenistic Period. Museo Archeologico. Syracuse, Italy. British Museum. **Bottom left.** Helmet with horses and lions. Bronze. Late seventh century B.C. Metropolitan Museum of Art, New York. **Bottom right.** Silver coins from Syracuse, Greece. Museo Archeologico. Sicily, Italy. **Page 15.** Lion. Marble. Circa 575 B.C. Delos, Greece. **Page 19.** *See cover.* **Page 20. Inset.** Spartan warrior. Sixth century B.C. **Page 22.** Riding dolphins. Mosaic. House of Dolphins. Delos, Greece.

Web Sites

Due to the changing nature of Internet links, PowerKids Press has developed an online list of Web sites related to the subject of this book. This site is updated regularly. Please use this link to access the list: www.powerkidslinks.com/psaciv/landgre/